Daisy Fried

The Year

Flood Editions, Chicago

the City

Emptied

After Baudelaire

I Have Not Forgotten

I have not forgotten, neighbor,
Our red brick rowhouse, tiny and quiet
With the window always cracked open
Even in winter, and us rolling together
Into the middle of the dented mattress,
A rooster in someone's courtyard crowing
In the gray, lording it over his harem
Of illegal chickens; where like gods
We couldn't stop being naked;
Those evenings the sun, superbly streaming,
Broke its sheaf of colors on the glass,
Seemed a giant inquisitive eye
Watching our long quiet suppers,
Its reflections spritzing like candlelight
On the frugal tablecloth
And on the strewn pages of your manuscripts.

—i.m. Jim Quinn (1935–2020)

Published by Flood Editions

www.floodeditions.com

ISBN 978-1-7332734-8-0

Cover illustration: Paula Rego, *Grooming*, 1994

Pastel on paper on aluminum, 29 × 39.4 inches

© Paula Rego, courtesy the artist and Victoria Miro

Design and composition by Crisis

Printed in Michigan on

acid-free, recycled paper

Contents

Foreword

I don't know French well and I don't like Baudelaire much—he oozes with decay, pestilence, death, and adjectives; is a tireless invoker of muses, classical figures, goddesses and personifications; is even more self-centered than me, and—have you ever counted how many times "azure" shows up in *Les Fleurs du mal*? But his disgust is glorious, and diagnostic, and he's always most revolted by himself. We in America could use more romantic self-disgust. Also, is there anything in poetry so terribly dry and so full of yearning as Baudelaire's "Le Cygne," a poem of his I probably love?

I started messing with Baudelaire by accident in spring, 2020. My husband was slowly dying of a cruel disease that attacked his body and mind, and he spent most of his time in a hospital bed in the living room. For quite a while, we didn't have help to speak of. For months we—by which I mean I, with legal advice—were fighting Medicaid, and then an insurance company Medicaid contracts with, to get them to pay for sufficient home-health-aide hours to make the time Jim had left a little more bearable. We got COVID too, mild cases, but it knocked us out for a time, and delayed what help we finally did get. There were other things, but that's enough whining for now. After all, we were all alive last spring, and as Jim said till quite far along, "It's always better to be alive."

I wasn't writing much new poetry. But one day I was stealing a rare few minutes for myself and pulled a book of John Ashbery translations from the French off the shelf. As I recall, I'd decided to read a few poems from each book in my library in alphabetical order, and had already been through Agudelo, Ai, Amichai, Ammons, and Anderson. Ashbery was next. (He killed the reading project because he gave me a writing one.) Not having the brain power just then for "... Convex Mirror ..." I turned straight to see what Baudelaire Ashbery had translated, for no particular reason other than that I'd read some Baudelaire in the past, limpingly in the original, and in inadequate translation. He'd done only one, "Paysage" ("Landscape"). Better than many, its English nonetheless chimed and bounced too much. "I can do better!" I thought, self-importantly, which is how, I assume, most translators start.

Jim wasn't feeling too bad that day, so I had longer than usual. I discovered when I'd gotten it pretty well done, that "Paysage" seemed very much a quarantine poem: Baudelaire alone in his attic, mob outside, dreaming of eternity. Best thing was, for the first time in a long time, I felt the pure joy of making and revising that finishing a poem brings—only without the grave difficulty of confronting a completely blank page to begin. Over the next weeks and months I tried another, and another, and each poem I did seemed to have something to say about life in 2020, about illness, about losing one's beloved, in a corrupt, violent, economically spiraling country led by an incompetent malignant narcissist, with its police and other institutions racist, its people in crisis.

I guess Baudelaire let me say things I wouldn't normally say, in ways I can't imagine writing in my own poems. More and more as I went, I shifted him towards twenty-first-century America, and/or towards my own idiom. I think most of these are recognizable as coming *from* Baudelaire, especially in the poems' imagery and structure. But I jettisoned adjectives, chose Germanic-origin words over Latinate, moved poems from Paris to Philly, and wrote as a woman (looking, for example, mostly at men, where Baudelaire did the opposite). I didn't stress about meter or end rhyme—that's where translators most often go wrong anyway. I'm sure—no, I hope—I got many things wrong about the French. I take that as an achievement. That year I had—I'd say, if I were writing this for social media—no fucks left to give. In that, I was, maybe, a little like Baudelaire in his own time. Strangely, across centuries and an ocean, it seemed we were in tune. *Je verrai les printemps, les étés, les automnes*, wrote Baudelaire in "Paysage": "I'll see spring-time, I'll see summer, and fall." And all through that time, Baudelaire helped me, enormously. Thanks, Charlie.

The Year

the City

Emptied

Baudelaire's "Paysage"

To compose my sexless eclogues, I will
Bed down near the sky like the astrologers
And, neighbor to bell towers, listen dreamily
To the somber wind-carried hymns.
Chin in hand, high up under the slant roof,
I'll see the factories' chatter and singsong,
Their chimneys and steeples, those masts of the city,
And the giant sky dreaming of eternity.

It's sweet, through mists, to watch a star
Born in the blue, lamp at the window,
Rivers of coal climbing the sky,
Moon pouring sorcery. Up there
I'll see springtime, I'll see summer, fall,
And when winter comes with monotone snow,
I'll close curtains and blinds
And build my fairy palaces in the night.
I'll dream of blue bright horizons,
Of gardens, of fountains crying in alabaster,
Of kisses, birds singing evening and morning—

All that infantile Idyll. And
When Riot storms impotent at my window,
I won't get up from my desk,
I'll be plunged, voluptuous,
In calling forth Spring by force of will,
Prising sunshine from my heart, making
Of my burning thoughts a gentler weather.

Daybreak

Helicopters sang out in the South Philly sky
And morning wind blew branches against our windows.

It was the hour my dream swarm
Twisted me pale on my pillow;
When like a bloodshot eye darting and twitching,
The last lamp stained the day incarnadine;
Where, trapped in my surly body
I recast the battle between lamp and day
As my struggle between intention and accident,
And like a face wiped dry by breezes,
The air was full of thrilling, fleeing things—
Anger, Change—
I was tired of writing, or you were,
You were tired of fucking, or I was.

This and that torched boutique sent up smoke.
Somebody heaved a planter into another store window.
The shopkeeper put the safety back on his sidearm,
With stinging eyes dialed his insurance adjuster.

Someone danced on a police car.
Someone blew up an ATM and his hand off with it.
Women who forgot to stop bearing children
Mopped their brows and chewed on ice,
It was the hour when, sweating and starving,
They gave birth to their latest moaning and cursing;
Like a sob cut short by foaming blood,
A siren, another, tore through the fabric of morning;
Buildings snuffled like marine mammals
Bedded down in smog sea.
Old ones in nursing homes, their minds gone,
Hawked up last juddering breaths.
They'd been abandoned
As I sometimes wish to abandon you.
Someone crept home, broken by stupidity.

Shivery Dawn in her green-pink shift
Crawls up the Schuylkill, into the parklands.
Angry Philly, rubbing her eyes,
Grabs up her tools again, that old worker.

Dr. No

Off to the side as if she's not leader,
Eyebrows penciled in,
Otherwise most fresh-faced,
Temperate, small baubles clicking
From her lobes, scent of rose water
Levitating from her clavicles,
In a poorly ventilated conference room
On industrial carpets,
Oozing commiseration,
Her teeth like peppermint chiclets.
Her job is *no*. She does her job.
Someone's got to.
It's a game. Her fame. House rigged to win.
Under a fluorescent ceiling
That washes me out,
Washes out the young lawyer come to help
Only to waste her time,
Behold my unspooling nightmare,
Me in the corner, mute till questioned,
Hot then cold then hot, answering

Her—in retrospect—funereal
Yet respectful-seeming questions,
Gabbling my elaborate, worried facts,
Rising up in me that guilty feeling
The roughly law-abiding get
When a cop draws up alongside
And turns his head to stare.
Behold her gallant solidarity
For the working woman—
Odd her rugged fingernails
When she raises her hand to take mine—
A couple of cuticles bleeding where she ripped them—
The picture of sympathy, but *no*.

—for Dr. C. S.

A Strange Engraving

This ghoul has, clamped to his cadaverous dome,
A diadem in the shape of a cone, signifying hate.
Without spurs or whip, he drives like a tank the pale horse,
Apocalyptic hack who drools from his nose
Like a snuffling cokehead. Through spacious skies
Together they thunder, trampling with hazardous hooves
The multitudes. A crackling and rattling of money.
A growl in the mind, moans from maws.
The rider with flaming tiki parades over crowds
His steed crushes, and, rooting out traitors to his cause,
Gallops over a graveyard nation
Where, stacked as far as the eye can see,
By fever light of a black sun, are body on body
Of those who perished by his bloody jobbery.

—for Stephen Miller

Obsession

Wilderness, you scare me like cathedrals,
You howl and rattle like organs.
My dark heart answers
... one season, the season of sorrow ...

Ocean, I loathe your bounding and tumult.
That's already in my beat brain.
Bitter hilarity, weeps and insults:
All I hear in the sniggering sea.

Night! Take down your stars.
I already know their language of light,
Want only black blankness.

But shadows themselves are sketchpads
Where live, by thousands, as under my eyelids,
Flickers and flashes of the dead.

Reader,

Blunders, errancy, avarice, and horseshit
Occupy my mind while training my body.
And shall I feed Cousin Remorse
As beggars feed amiable vermin?

Here's fake penance for my sins.
I'm paid handsomely for my confessions,
And choose, giddy always, the swamp.
Crocodile tears shall washeth my stains,

Satan's pillow rock me,
My sterling will evaporate.
Devil who holds my strings:
Dance me towards repulsive things.

Daily, hellward, clandestine, I descend
Step by step, lured by lurid stench,
Horny, propositioning boys for sale,
Squeezing to get nectar from that fruit,

Serried, swarming, like a million tapeworms
In the brain, populace demonic,
And when I breathe, I believe I breathe
Death, that invisible river of lamenting.

Rape, arson, poniard, venom (Exhibits A–D):
If I've not yet stitched their pleasant designs
Into our banal canvas, dismal destiny,
It's only because my soul's too chicken—

But among jackals, panthers, apes, and lice,
Scorpions, snakes, vultures, all
The ravening fiends who growl and crawl
In the infamous zoo of my vices,

The ugliest, nastiest, filthiest
Doesn't tap dance, lap dance, or catcall.
She'd gladly turn the earth to rubble
And yawning swallow us:

Listlessness! She of the gummy eyes,
Dreaming of the gallows while sucking at her bong.
You know her, reader, this delicate monster—
Hypocrite reader—doppelganger—sister!

The Soul of Wine

One night, wine sang in the bottles:
"O woman disowned, from my prison of glass
And red sealing wax, to you I give
A song of light and sisterhood.

I know how, on the flaming fell,
It takes murderous toil under a baking sun
To give me life and soul.
Gratitude. To you I won't be vicious:

Such joy to tumble down the throat
Of a woman like you, exhausted by work.
Your warm belly's my sweet rest:
Better pleasure there than in the cold vault.

Can you hear sabbath canticles
Singing out in my breast, sobbing with hope?
Elbows plunked on table, sleeves rolled,
Worship me and be contented,

I'll ignite your ravished husband's eyes;
To your daughter I'll return luster and mettle
And be for her, frail wrestler of life,
The oil for her muscles.

Into you I—fruity ambrosia—fall,
Precious seed sown by the Sower,
So from our amour grows poetry,
Spurting towards God like a flower."

Baudelaire's Cats

1.

Cat, come,

Sleek bewitcher,

Retract your claws

Into your paw pads.

Let me sink

In your beautiful eyes

Meld of metal

And agate.

When my fingers

Caress your nape

And supple back,

And my hand

Gets drunk

With the pleasure

Of touching

Your electric body,

I think of my man.

His stare, like yours, beast,

Deep, cold, cut

And split like a dart,
And head to foot
A subtle air,
A dangerous scent,
Swims around
His unknowable
Body.

2.

Lover or scholar,

Older, you admire

Cat sweetness

And cat power,

Pride of the home.

Gone torpid

And gun-shy

You sit by

The fire.

Familiar of science

And of pleasure,

He keeps to the dark side:

Silence. Horror.

Devil wants him

As doom-steed—

As if he could sell

Himself for that serfdom.

Behold, he muses

In poses of sphinxes

Lonely in the desert,
Submerged
In endless dream;
His loins are aglitter
With magic sparks
Like yours were;
And gold patches,
And fine sharp sand,
Star his mystic eyes.

3.

Through my brain,
Like it's his own backyard,
Strolls my charming cat,
His noise is profound, plush
And pearly, infiltrates
My darkest deeps,
Complicates like good poetry,
Settles me like a pill. He says
The manifold, needful things
Without a word, lullabies
My ecstasies of worry,
And thus as if with catgut bow,
Tunes my heart, his instrument.
From his motley fur
Comes a perfume so sweet
That one evening I thought
I was embalmed in it, having
Caressed him one time—
Just the once! He judges,

Presides, he inspires
All things in his empire.
Is he gremlin? Is he god?
Who shall say he is not
The happy genius of his household?
For when my eyes, obedient
To this cat I love, are pulled to him
As towards a magnet
I look inside myself.
Clear lanterns, pale eye-fire,
Living opals, fix me.

Loving Lies

When I see you passing, lazybones mine,
Songsound of the band breaking on my ceiling,
And you pause your leisurely stroll
To look peaceably about, airing your ennui;

When I think, entranced by the way the strobe
Brings color to your faded face
Like evening torches still lit at dawn,
Your eyes like the stoned ones of *Women of Algiers*,

I say to myself: "Gorgeous! Yet eerily cool . . ."
Memory's a citadel; massive,
It crowns him, and his heart, a bruised peach,
Is ripe, like his body, for a tale of love.

Are you the autumn fruit, full-flavored, mature?
Urn of ashes waiting for my tears,
Incense redolent of distant oases,
Soft pillow, or flower basket?

I know there are eyes which, melancholy,
Give up their secrets; inlaid boxes
Missing their jewels, relics gone from lockets
Emptier, profounder than you, dark sky.

But isn't it enough that your looks
Make my heart, fleeing from truth, rejoice?
Brainless, indifferent—what does it matter?
Mask, or wallpaper—hey! I adore your body . . .

Jewels

My man gets naked and, knowing my hunger,
The family jewels are all he wears.
This gives him an air of opulence,
Playing stud in the seraglio, and

When he dances, virile and mocking,
He seems made of a world of rock and steel,
So that I may in beguiled fury adore
His whole body, paunch and luster.

So he's lying there, letting himself be loved
And from the top of the chaise, smirks
With pleasure at my lust, deep and sweet
As the ocean that, tidal, climbs a cliff.

His eyes on me are a barely tamed tiger's.
He plays vague and dreamy, strikes poses
Of animal lust and ravishment,
Satisfying me with every twist and thrust.

And his arms and leg, and his thigh and ass,
Polished like oil, pumping like the neck of a swan,
Pass before me, and now I feel . . . becalmed?
And his belly and his—clusters and vine . . .

Advance, then, tempter,
Disturb my soul's repose, my Zen,
Lure me from my crystalline calm
Where I thought I might, lonely, rest awhile.

And now I swear I can see Apollo
United to Priapus in hairy chest, bit of a belly,
And below, his narrow dressy pelvis:
The tawny textures are superb.

And the lamp has resigned itself to die,
And the flickering hearth barely lights the room,
And every time he sighs his sigh,
He swamps us both with his electricity.

Temper

Revolutionary Rain, pissed at the world,
Slops cold sop in spouts from his flask
On the dead in the neighboring burial grounds
And fear of death on the misty in-burbs.

My cat scritches the rug—needs to shit.
His skinny body shakes
As Poet Rain bumbles in the gutters,
Dismal old ghoul.

The droning bell laments, furnace stutters,
Falsetto accompaniment to the sick clock,
And in my stinking card deck

(Souvenir of a man with swollen ankles)
Jack of Hearts (*hawt!*) prattles with Queen Heads-on-Pikes
Of their defunct tyrannical adulteries.

Temper

I got more crap up here than if I lived a thousand years.

A filing cabinet stuffed with credit-card statements,
Doggerel, "love" letters, subpoenas, paperback novels,
Heavy locks of sex partners' hair folded up in paper,
Hides fewer secrets than my blasted brain.
It's a mausoleum, enormous walk-in freezer,
Holds more dead than a mass grave.
I'm a graveyard the moon hates,
Where remorse is the tunneling worm
Chomping through my dearest departeds.
I'm an old bedroom stuffed with wilted roses,
Strewn with last year's castoff fashions,
Where sick pastels of fatted Boucher babies
Stink of talc and the open bottle.

The limping days are so fucking long
Snowed under by years and years and years and years.
Say it: Boredom born of apathy
Achieves immortality. Body, you're nothing:

Bag of dread and granite crag, magma cooled,
Old sphinx in a fog, mumbling to self,
Forgotten by the whole giddy world,
Haranguing in the dwindling light.

Temper

I'm like the Provost they used to call rainmaker,
Endowed but impotent, gleaming but spent,
Disdaining lecturers lickspittling his boots
As you might be bored with puppies! and all other beasts.
Nothing can cheer him—no promotion or publication,
Nor students demonstrating in front of his window.
His favorite admin, grotesquely singing his praises,
No longer amuses. Tbh, he's twisted and sick.
His stand-up desk resembles a sarcophagus;
The suck-ups, for whom all bosses are beautiful,
No longer know how to please,
Elicit no simper from his manscaped face.
His chief alchemist in HR hasn't been able
To leach out tainting corruption; they tried
Furloughing full-timers—the Bloodbath
They called it—failed to restore institutional health.
He doesn't know how to warm his dazed brains.
Nothing but buzzwords running in his veins.

Temper

When pewter sky clamps like a lid
On my trouble-flooded mind,
Girdling my city to the horizon,
Days are bitterer than the nights;

When Earth's a dank prison
And Hope beats at the walls
With papery wings, and enfeebled,
Hangs from rotten rafters;

When rain trailing ensigns and streamers
Descends like a jail grille
And the people all are poison spiders
Spreading their nets in my brain,

And the bells in my head start lunging with fury,
Yelping to the cloud cover,
Stumbling, desperado, off their meds,
Subsiding to muttered curses,

—Then long hearses, with no dirge or backbeat,
Roll through my soul. Then Hope
Folds; black Anguish
Stabs its anarchist pennant through my skull.

Hate Barrel

Hate's a wine barrel from which I glug,
Turning me into Madam Vengeance with beefy raw arms
Rushing ridiculous to hurl slop-buckets of blood
And tears of the dead into the onslaught of lies.

Poke holes in their myths
And out fly centuries of toil and anguish.
Hate revives his victims,
Resurrecting us—to bleed us again.

Hate's a drunk in the stickiest dive,
Its thirst gives birth to thirst
That multiplies like Hydra's heads.

But lucky drunks know their oppressor
Hate's doomed to a dismal fate:
Dumbass can't even pass out under the table.

Music

Music like a sea!
Under ceiling of mist,
To my pale star
I set sail
In clear air.

Breathing huge and deep
Like the canvas of a ship
I mount the backs
Of rollers.
May night veil me.

Breeze, gust,
Storm convulsion:
Derelict ship, I vibrate
Soft feelings, mega emotions.

Immense abyss,
Lull and lullaby me.
Doldrums,
Mirror my despair!

Auto Autumn

In the mirror, my own clear eyes say
"What, strange lover, is my merit?"
Shut up and charm me. Everything irks me
But primitive animal candor. My heart

Would hide its nasty secret,
Living lullaby whose hand strokes me to deep sleep,
Would conceal its fire-dark bedtime story.
I hate sex. It makes me sick.

Then let's love coolly. Cupid waits
in dark ambush, bending deadly crossbow.
I know the machines of his ancient arsenal:

Crime and loathing and madness!—oh pale flower,
Aren't you, like me, the sun in November?
So white, so cold, my Daisy?

Autumn Song

Soon the plunge in dark and cold;
Goodbye too soon to summer's limpid light!
Already, I'm hearing firewood thump
Its hollow pavement shocks.

Winter feelings rush in: wrath,
Loathing, thrills of dread, sentence of hard labor,
And, like the sky in its polar hell,
My heart will freeze, a meaty block.

I shudder, listening to each log chopped.
A gallows being built has that muffled echo.
My mind's a teetering parapet
Annihilated by a battering ram below.

Rockabyed by this metronomic knock,
Seems someone hasty's nailing shut a coffin—
For whom?—it was just summer! now fall.
This odd noise rings out like loss.

*

I love the green light in your long eyes,
Comely one, but today I'm bitter,
And nothing, not our love, or bed, or hearth,
Is worth sunlight dappling the sea.

But darling! adore me. Be my daddy—
I'll be your naughty ingrate—
Or anyway, lover, brother, be the passing amity
Of autumn glory, setting sun.

Quick work. The greedy tomb awaits.
Ah, let me kneel, head resting on your knees,
To taste—grieving for burning summer—
These good late mellow yellow rays.

Owls

In black yew shelters,
Owls tuck themselves away,
Strange gods
With red meditating shifty eyes,

Otherwise roost unstirring
Till the melancholy hour
When darkness shovels
The sun offstage.

Thus, they teach the sage
She need fear in this world
Only tumult and action.

Passing, drunk on shadows,
My punishment for desiring change
Is desiring more change.

Baudelaire's "Le Soleil"

In an old faubourg where, hanging from hovels,
Jalousies hide languorous lust,
When cruel sun redoubles its drubbing
Of city and field, rooftop and wheat crop,
I'll joust out my loner fantasy,
Sniffing rhymes from every corner,
Tripping on words as over cobblestones,
To chance verses no one has ever dreamed.

Foster father, foe to anemia, the sun
Raises worms and roses like verses in the fields,
Burns off care like mist to the sky,
Fills our minds and hives with honey.
It's he who lifts the spirits of men with crutches
Making them sweet and gay as girls,
And orders the harvest to ripen and thrive
In the immortal heart, all's desperate to bloom.

When, like a poet, he goes down in the cities,
He dignifies the grubbiest, vilest things,
And, relinquishing fanfare and servants, like a king
Inspects all the pesthouses and mansions.

Cataract

How like steam escaping the boil
Were your blurry eyes—what color are they?
By turns tender, dreamy, and cruel
With the pallor and indolence of the sky.

I remember white days of long haze
When, ravished and twisted by nerves,
I wept, my melting mind split in two;
My waking and sleeping mocked each other.

Sometimes you seemed a gorgeous horizon
That suns in seasons of fog set afire
As, rainy landscape, you shone
Dappled by rays breaking through blur.

Dangerous Man, *Hombre*, Mister Languor,
Shall I learn now to adore your frosts and snow,
Shall I get from this relentless winter
Pleasures that sting like tongue touched to iron?

White on White

Bored, our crew traps albatross,
Great birds of the deeps,
Lazy fellow travelers
Of vessels sliding above the bitter chasm.

The minute we lay them out on the boards,
These piteous kings of the azure,
Awkward and ashamed, splay,
Like oars, their white massive wings.

Winged wayfarer! Gauche. Stupid.
Was lovely, now ludicrous, and foul.
I stuff my lit pipe in its beak.
Another mocks its crippled step.

Sky-poet, prince of clouds
Who haunts the storm and laughs at hunters,
Grounded amid hoots and mocks, can't walk.
What lifted you smacks you flat.

Invitation in Hospice

Child, brother:
Let's dream of a sweet thing:
Of living together, forever
Loving and dying in that country
So like you, where after downpour
The clouds go scrambling
Out of the way of late sunshine
Like your wicked,
Bright, tear-clouded eyes.
Everything's luxury,
Voluptuous calm, there. There, nothing
But order and beauty.
The years would polish
Our tables and sideboards,
The jade vine and ghost orchid mingle,
Odor of amber, faint, collecting
In the ceiling's mahogany coffers,
Magnificent mirrors, beveled
And chamfered. Everything speaks
In our secret sweet tongue.

Order, calm, etc. Your body.
On the canals, look:
Houseboats, drowsing,
Mood vagabond, drifted here
From world's end to satisfy
Your least desire. The setting sun
Clothes fields, waterways,
The whole city in hyacinth, hyacinth and in gold.
Our world would slumber in that light.
There forever, voluptuous calm,
Order, beauty.

The Broken Bell

I like, winter nights, to find in a heat lamp
That beats and fumes, old memories
Rising in the banging
Of church bells through snow spray.

Blessed be the bell of liberty
That, ancient, keeps trying to ring,
Tossing out his faithful cry
Like an old soldier in his bunker

On the eve of battle. My soul's broken,
And when I want songs of trouble,
It often happens that his voice weakens

Like the death rattle of a forgotten man
By a lake of blood, under a pile of the dead,
Who dies, without moving, in struggle.

The Goose

Andromache—widow—fighter of men—
I think of you by the poor mirror
Of the river which glitters with grieving,
Seems to show by its slow full float

The size of our sadness. It seeds my memory.
Walking where the road carousels,
Everything bewilders, a city changes!
Faster than a human heart. That's a field.

There, houses. And the grasses: green blocks
Where water puddled. Upriver, a zoo,
Giraffes hung their faces over a wall.
We took our girl, arriving early, the hour

The air was cold and clear; there I live
In memory. And here I live, Andromache,
In the dull what-is. Then sweaty work wakens,
Traffic awakens to make of the silence

A dark hurricane, and there's a goose . . .
Separated from its hateful shitting gaggle
That marauds by the boathouses,
Rasps webs over the macadam,

Dodges fast cars. His stained hind plumage
Trails on the ground, he shambles
Near the disc of the enormous fountain—
Dry and silent since disease broke on us,

Dry since the city emptied itself of itself,
Emptied its people only to rooms.
Dry the bronze breasts of the river spirit statues,
The birdshit-stained spouting bronze swans

They hoist on their shoulders, dry-mawed.
As if the ruins of a beloved, his broken cornices,
Sprawled stone blocks stained green,
Can be forgotten. No kids playing there

Nor older folks coming back to ill-advised life
For an early dark morning drunken grope.
Nope. Just the living goose
Nervously bathing wings in brimming filth—

Scum, dung, rotten leaves. He opens his beak,
Heart full of his native lake he'll never return to,
As if to say, "Water, when will you rain?
Sky, when lightning, thunder?"

Unlucky bird, son of the sun,
You stretch your pumping neck up and up
Toward the hazy azure as if like me
You're blaming God who doesn't exist.

*

Our Philly changes, I wander back
Into glass canyons between unleasable
New office towers, and in their bases
Shuttered shops with bric-a-brac

Displayed unbought in ghastly windows,
Empty bars and restaurants, their outdoor tables
Barely inhabited, heat-lamp flames
Warming air where people aren't.

Trucks hitting wrinkle bumps; distant sirens,
Sirens, sirens; scaffolding, rehabs paused,
Old mini-mansions, roofs fallen in,
Laborers for insurance law firms

Hunched at screens, working for the market,
Everything metaphor
For memories heavier than rocks.
Outside the Rodin Museum,

Images oppress me. Dour Thinker
And Gates of Hell. And my great goose
With his crazy motions, and then you,
Andromache, ridiculous, sublime,

Like and not at all like the protestors
In their playing-field encampment of nylon
And polyester in teals and grays, pegged with cords
To tired trees, with laundry hung between

And *Black Lives Matter* and other signs,
No Cop Zone, *Housing Now*, *Our Demands!*:
Long list. Some sit stoned, some march about.
The grass remains a stretch of emerald.

I don't want to say I'm gnawed by longing
For a man like a city, city like a man
Whose mind's a ruined city—
I'm bored with these feelings they call grief.

Andromache, fighter, your husband ripped from you,
You felt a captive beast, wandering deserted streets,
Heavy, aching, widow of the world.
One protestor emerged from the mass,

Tripped on a tent wire, and crying
Cursed into a bullhorn, muttered something
About a mama hugging, soothing them,
Keeping them safe. And the man I love said

You think my eyes are pretty? Oh,
You should have seen my mother's eyes.
They were the most beautiful blue—
The last most lucid thing he said to me.

Old memory like a lost goose vanishing
Honks out a full note. What good to think
Of others forgotten, kneeled-on, jailed, killed,
Defeated, robbed . . . ? so many others more.

Twilight

Silk evening, criminals' accomplice,
Comes padding like a wolf, sky
Clicking shut like a crypt—
Restless we turn into beasts.

Oh night, craved by us
Whose arms can honestly say: "Today
We've worked!"—night solaces
The soul devoured by mad grief,
The stubborn scientist bowing his head,
The stooped worker returning to bed.
But too: demons corrupt the atmosphere,
Waking hungover like stockbrokers,
Their fly-by knocking eaves and shutters,
While under wind-tormented gas lamps
Hustlers take the glimmering streets
Like an anthill, they open for business,
Clear roads and networks,
An enemy getting ready.
They move in our city's filth,

Worms who strip men's flesh and eat.
Here and there, a kitchen hisses,
Theater yelps, orchestra grinds and snores.
The buffet at the casino, where games delight,
Fills up with hookers and sharps, all that scum,
And merciless thieves
Prepare for their nightly routine
Of forcing doors and cracking safes,
To fund a few more nights with their bejeweled whores.

Collect yourself, self, in this dark time.
Close your ears to the mayhem.
This is the hour the sick suffer most!
Black night takes their throats; fate
Rushes them towards their final nothingness.
The hospital is filled with their suffocating sighs.
No more aromas of soup by the fire,
Evenings with the beloved.

But how many have never known
The sweetness of home: have never lived.

Correspondences

Our woods today was a temple where living pillars
Whispered leaf-words, bark-words; a woman
Passing there crosses a forest of symbols
In the lichens, the mosses, schist on the hillside,
Which watch her with knowing glances.
Like faraway echoes
Their shadowy, complex entwining
Was vast as night in the clear light of day
In the deepnesses between trees
And the chasm the creek carved,
So your smells, colors, the sounds you made—
I remember them—correspond:
Scents fresh as infant skin, sweet as oboes,
Prairie-green—
And others, mulchy and rich,
Becoming compost, expanding infinite
As amber, musk, resin, and incense
To sing the soarings of my spirit and senses.

* * *

Notes and Acknowledgments

"Baudelaire's 'Paysage'" and "Baudelaire's 'Le Soleil'" are close enough to the originals to be called translations. "Dr. No" initially used Baudelaire's "Le Jeu" as pretext, but it is hardly even at this point a version. All others are "after Baudelaire," and their originals, which can easily be read at fleursdumal.org, are as follows:

I Have Not Forgotten	*Je n'ai pas oublié*
Daybreak	*Le Crépuscule du matin*
A Strange Engraving	*Une Gravure fantastique*
Obsession	*Obsession*
Reader,	*Au Lecteur*
The Soul of Wine	*L'Âme du vin*
Baudelaire's Cats	*Le Chat, Les Chats, Le Chat*
Loving Lies	*L'Amour du mensonge*
Jewels	*Les Bijoux*
Temper (1–4)	*Spleen (1–4)*
Hate Barrel	*Le Tonneau de la haine*
Music	*La Musique*
Auto Autumn	*Sonnet d'automne*
Autumn Song	*Chant d'automne*
Owls	*Les Hiboux*

Cataract	*Ciel brouillé*
White on White	*L'Albatros*
Invitation in Hospice	*L'Invitation au voyage*
The Broken Bell	*La Cloche fêlée*
The Goose	*Le Cygne*
Twilight	*Le Crépuscule du soir*
Correspondences	*Correspondances*

*

Dr. No is dedicated to Dr. C. S., a family-medicine practitioner who (presumably) makes extra cash presiding over an insurance-company panel that turns down disabled people's requests for help. Baudelaire's "Le Jeu," about a courtesan at a gaming table, was the original pretext, although this poem has moved far from the original. For one thing, Baudelaire admires his courtesan.

A Strange Engraving borrows some of its imagery from a political cartoon in the Star-Tribune by Steve Sack. https://www.startribune.com/sack-cartoon-trump-and-stephen-miller/565301912/

Obsession: Baudelaire's original line 4 is "Répondent les échos de vos *De Profundis*." I substituted Oscar Wilde, from his *De Profundis.*

Baudelaire's Cats: In part 3 I adapted lines from Williams' "Danse Russe" ("Who shall say I am not / the happy genius of my household?") and substituted them for Baudelaire's original quatrain ("C'est l'esprit familier du lieu; / Il juge, il préside, il inspire / Toutes choses dans son empire; / Peut-être est-il fée, est-il dieu?").

Loving Lies: Line 8 of the original is "Et tes yeux attirants comme ceux d'un portrait" ("And your eyes attract like those of a portrait"). I thought of Delacroix, whom Baudelaire revered and championed.

Jewels: "Les Bijoux" was originally censored for being likely to "lead to the excitement of the senses by a crude realism offensive to public decency."

Auto Autumn: The original is addressed to "Marguerite" (my real name, Margaret, translates to my nickname, Daisy). Baudelaire often writes like a perimenopausal woman looking in the mirror.

Baudelaire's "Le Soleil": While my French is weak and my understanding of French hardly idiomatic, it appears that "vers" can be translated as "verses" or "worms" and the word appears twice in this poem. In line 8—"des vers depuis longtemps rêvés"—it seems unlikely Baudelaire is dreaming of worms (though if any poet did it would be him). In line 10, it seems like worms are being raised by the sun. James McGowan translates it as "Wakes in the fields the worms as well as roses." I thought about having the sun raise the "worms like roses" but I decided that even if I'm incorrect, *worms, verses,* and *roses* should all appear in a single line.

The Goose: It turns out the name Andromache (Baudelaire addresses the famously loyal wife and widow in "Le Cygne") means, in its etymology, "fighter of men."

*

Gratitude to the editors of *Global Poemic, The Nation, On the Seawall, Paris Review, PN Review, Subtropics, The Summerset Review, Threepenny Review,* and *Zocalo Public Square,* where some of these poems first appeared.

Thank you and love to Sebastian Agudelo, August Kleinzahler, John McAuliffe, and of course Devin Johnston, who read and commented on all of these poems before they were published; and to Richard Adler, Nathalie Anderson, Melissa Silverman Backes, Miriam Fried, Ange Mlinko, Gail Orr, Tom Orr, Glorious Piner, Maisie Quinn, Alan Shapiro, Connie Voisine, and Eleanor Wilner, who read and commented on some or many of them. Thanks to Janell DuBois, Genae Felix, Kadija Kamara,

Antonine Lovely, Precious Mansaray, Nadia Soumahoro, Faith Speaks, Sarina Stewart, Samaria Turner, and Tyesha Turner of ComForCare Home Care, and to Nefertiti Childrey of Penn-Care, whose work made it possible for me to spend time on this project; same for Allison Schilling, Kate Vengraitis, and Pam Walz of Community Legal Services-Philadelphia, without whom we might have drowned. Jim Quinn listened to as many of these poems as he could, and it was his idea, early on, that I make them into a book. So I did.